Table of Contents
Phonics
Preschool

P9-DCI-477

School Specialty Publishing

Copyright © 2006 School Specialty Publishing. Published by Brighter Child®, an imprint of School Specialty Publishing, a member of the School Specialty Family.

Send all inquiries to:
School Specialty Publishing
8720 Orion Place
Columbus, OH 43240-2111

ISBN 0-7696-7619-7

3 4 5 6 7 8 9 10 WAL 09 08 07

COLORS

Name_____

Draw a line to match each picture to the crayon with the same color.

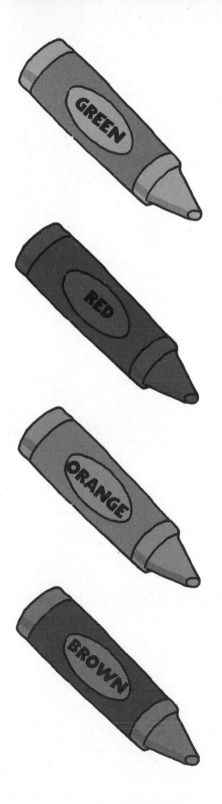

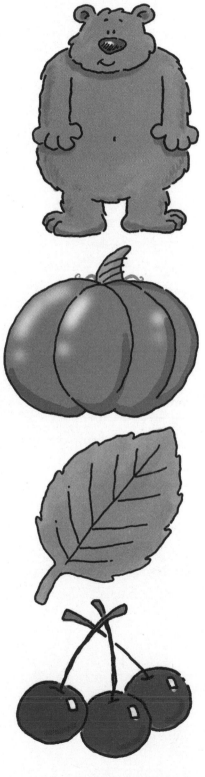

COLORS

In each row, color two things that are the same color.

SHAPES

Name_____

Trace the **circles**.

Trace the word.

circle

5

SHAPES

Trace the **squares**.

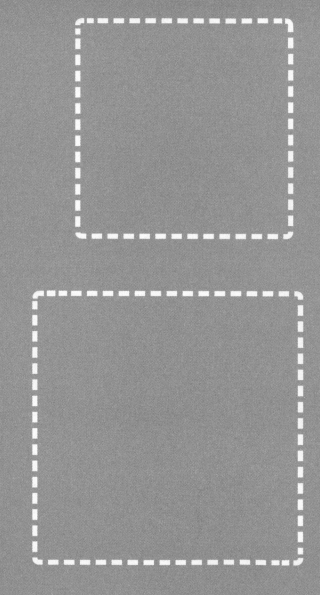

Trace the word.

square

6

SHAPES

Trace the **triangles**.

Trace the word.

triangle

SHAPES

Name _____

Trace the **rectangles**.

Trace the word.

rectangle

Circle the shape in each row that is the **same size** as the first shape.

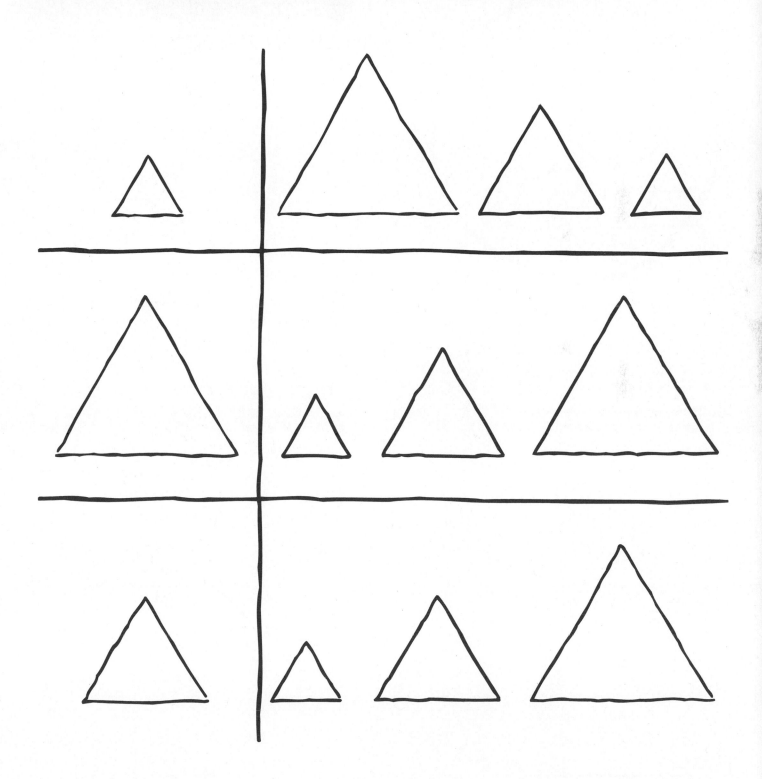

BIG AND SMALL

Name_____

Draw a line to match the shapes that are the same. Then color each **big** shape red and each **small** shape green.

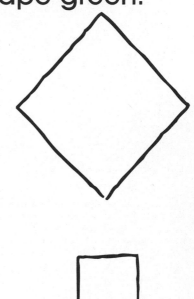

OPPOSITES

Look at the pictures in each row. Circle the picture that is the opposite of the first picture in each row.

GO-TOGETHERS

Look at the pictures in each row. Circle the picture that goes together with the first picture.

Name_____

SAME

Name_____

Look at the picture in each row. Circle the picture that is the **same** as the first picture in each row.

 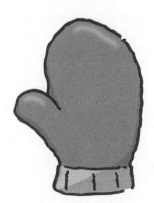 

Phonics: Grade Preschool

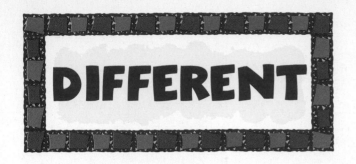

Name_____

Look at the pictures in each row. Circle the picture that is **different** in each row.

Look at the shapes in each row. Color the shape that is the **same** as the first shape in each row.

15

DIFFERENT

Name_____

Color the shape in each row that is **different**.

SAME

Name_____

Look at the letters in each row. Circle the letter that is the **same** as the first letter in each row.

E   F   E

R   B   R

M   M   N

SAME

Look at the letters in each row. Circle the letter that is the **same** as the first letter in each row.

u | u   n

d | b   d

h | h   n

18

Aa

Color the **A**'s **red**.
Color the **a**'s **green**.
Color the other letters **yellow**.

a c a

A A o

Bb

Name_____

Color to find the hidden picture.
- Color the spaces with **B blue**.
- Color the spaces with **b yellow**.
- Color the other spaces with a color you like.

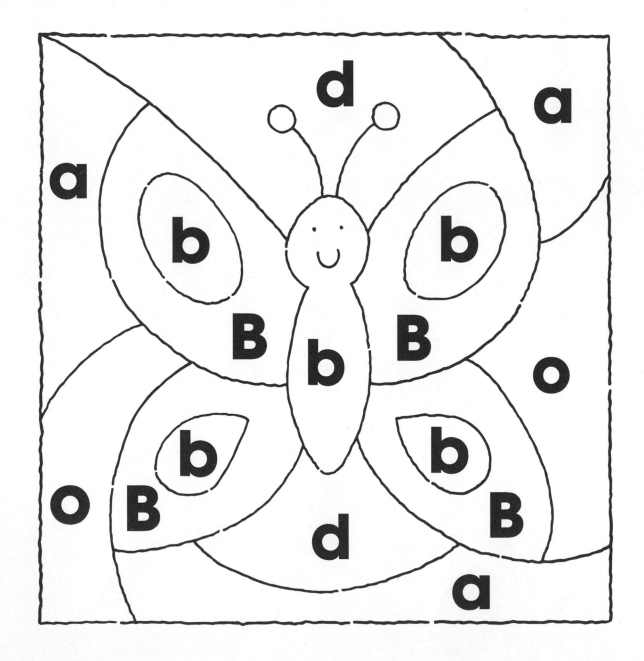

What did you find? _____

Cc

Name_____

Look at the patterns on the cats' sweaters. Draw a line between the cats with matching **Cc** patterns on their sweaters.

Phonics: Grade Preschool

LETTER REVIEW

Look at the letter each person is holding. Circle the same letter in each box.

D d

Name_____

Help the dolphin jump through the rings. Color the rings that have the letter **D** or **d** in them.

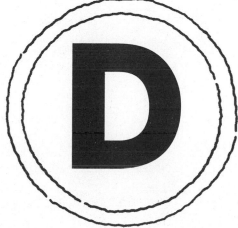

23

Phonics: Grade Preschool

Name_____

Help the baby elephant get to its mother. Color the footprints with **E** or **e** on them.

Name_____

LETTER REVIEW

Trace the letters on the caterpillar. Write the missing letters where they belong.

Phonics: Grade Preschool

Ff

Color the fish in the fish bowl.
- Color the **F** fish **orange**.
- Color the **f** fish **green**.
- Color the other fish with a color you like.

Gg

Name_____

Color to find the hidden picture.
- Color the spaces with **G yellow**.
- Color the spaces with **g brown**.

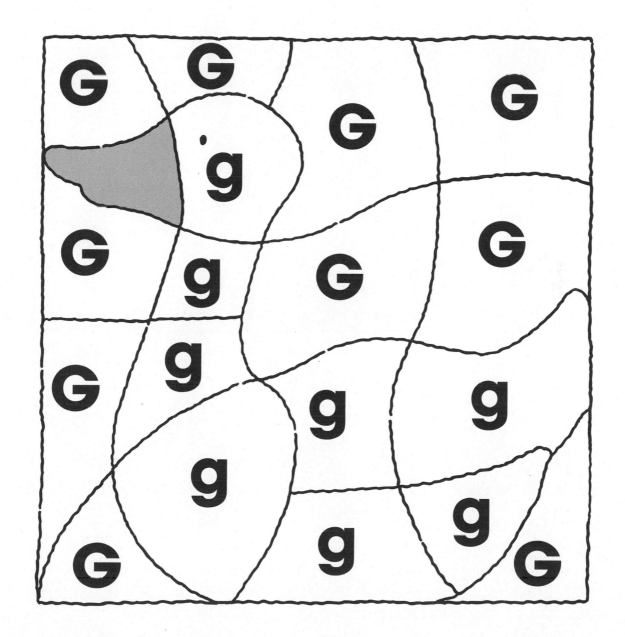

What did you find? _____

27

Color to find the hidden picture.

- Color the spaces with **H blue**.
- Color the spaces with **h brown**.

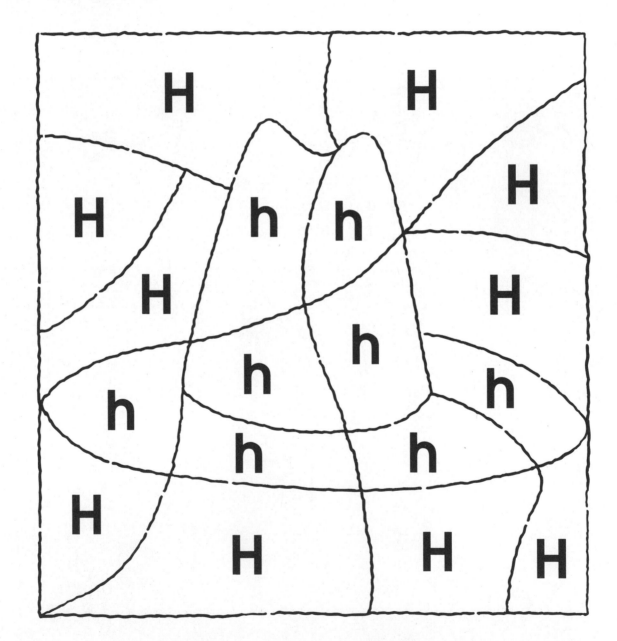

What did you find? _____

Ii

Help build the igloo. Trace the letters **I** and **i** below.

29

LETTER REVIEW

Trace the letters on the teddy bears. Write the missing letters where they belong.

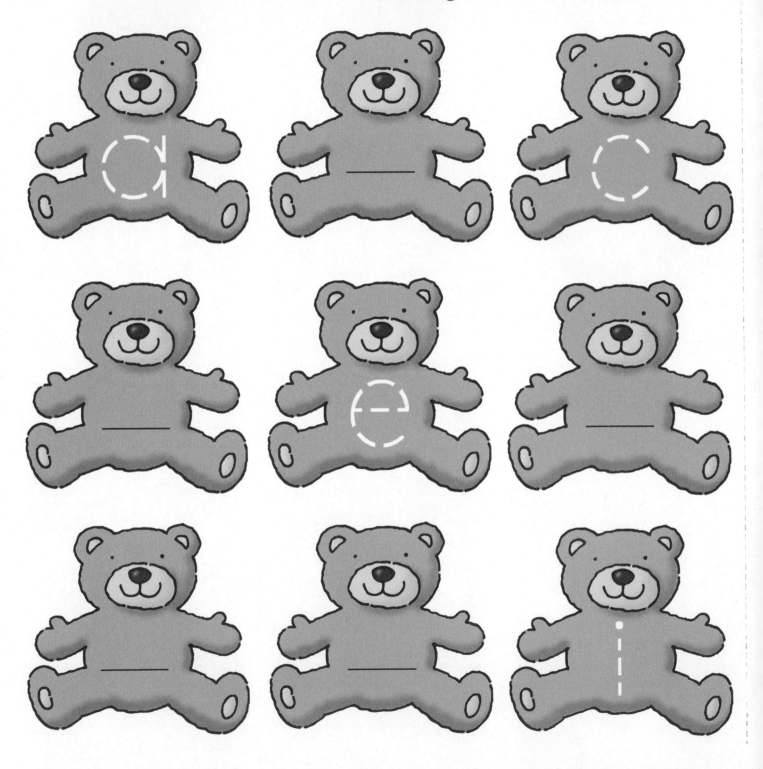

J j

Name_____

Jim has a ticket for a ride. Color to find the hidden picture.

- Color the spaces with **J** or **j** **blue**.
- Color the other spaces **gray**.

What will Jim ride in? _____

Kk

Name_____

Look at the letters on each key and lock. Draw a line between the keys and locks with matching letters.

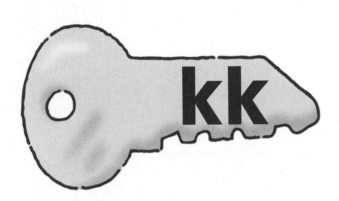

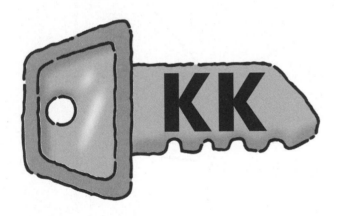

LETTER REVIEW

Name_____

Draw a line from each UPPERCASE letter to its matching lowercase letter.

J

H

K

I

Phonics: Grade Preschool

Letter
Ll

Name_____

It is fun to rake the fall leaves!

Color the leaves with **L** orange. **Color** the leaves with **l red**.

Mm

Color to find the hidden picture.
- Color the spaces with **M gray**.
- Color the spaces with **m yellow**.
- Color the other spaces with a color you like.

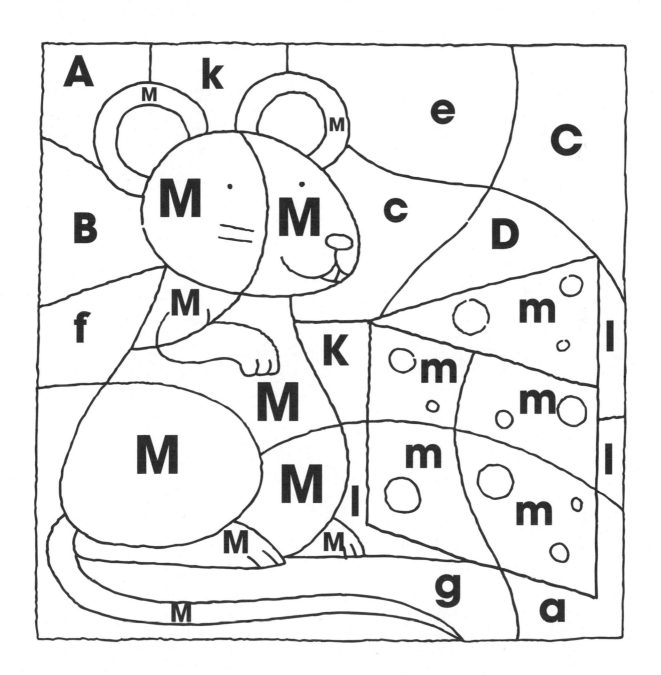

Letter Nn

Can you find each **N** and **n** that is hidden in the room?

Color each **N purple** and each **n orange**. Then **color** the rest of the room!

Name_____

What did the octopus see on the ocean floor?

- Color the spaces with **O** or **o** **blue**.
- Color the other spaces **brown**.

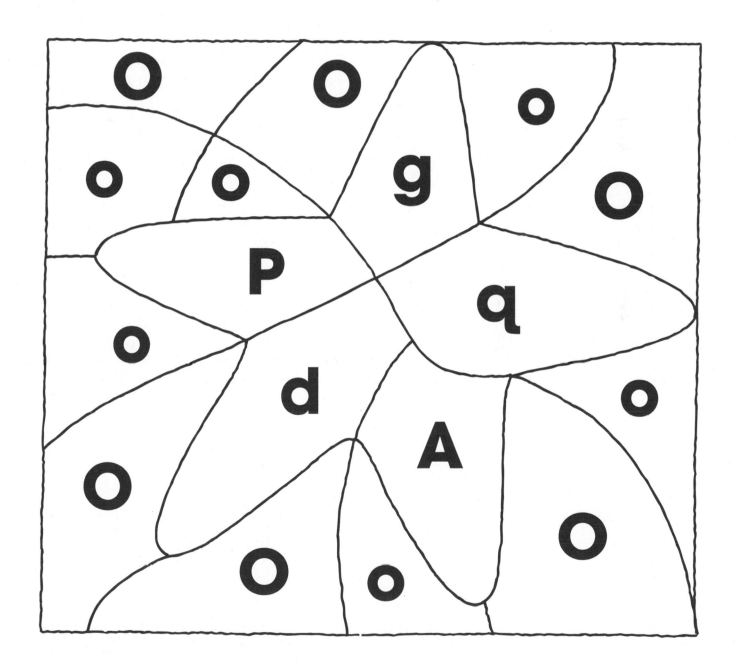

What did the octopus see?_____

37 *Phonics: Grade Preschool*

Letter Pp

Name_____

Color each **P** or **p** on the pizza **red**. Then **color** the rest of the pizza.

LETTER REVIEW

Name_____

Connect the dots as you say the alphabet from **A** to **P**. Then color the picture.

Name_____

Color the quilt.
- Color the squares with **Q green**.
- Color the squares with **q pink**.

Name_____

Trace each **R** and **r**. **Color** each raindrop with **R green**. **Color** each raindrop with **r blue**. Use the same colors for the letters on the umbrella.

Look at the letter patterns on the shirts and shorts. Draw a line from each shirt to the pair of shorts with the same letter pattern.

SsS

sSS

Sss

SsS

sSS

Sss

Name_____

Do you like to play tic-tac-toe?

Color each **T** and **t** with the correct color.
Draw a line to win tic-tac-toe.

T = red
t = green

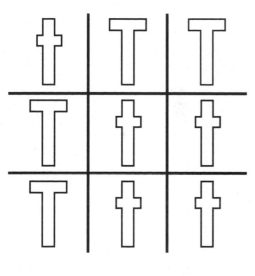

T = blue
t = yellow

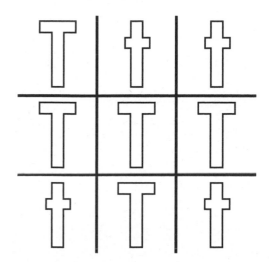

T = purple
t = orange

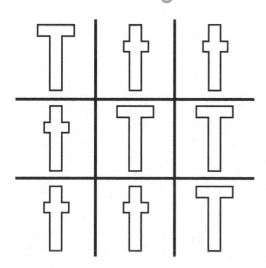

43

Phonics: Grade Preschool

LETTER REVIEW

Trace the letters on the blocks. Write the missing letters where they belong below and on page 45.

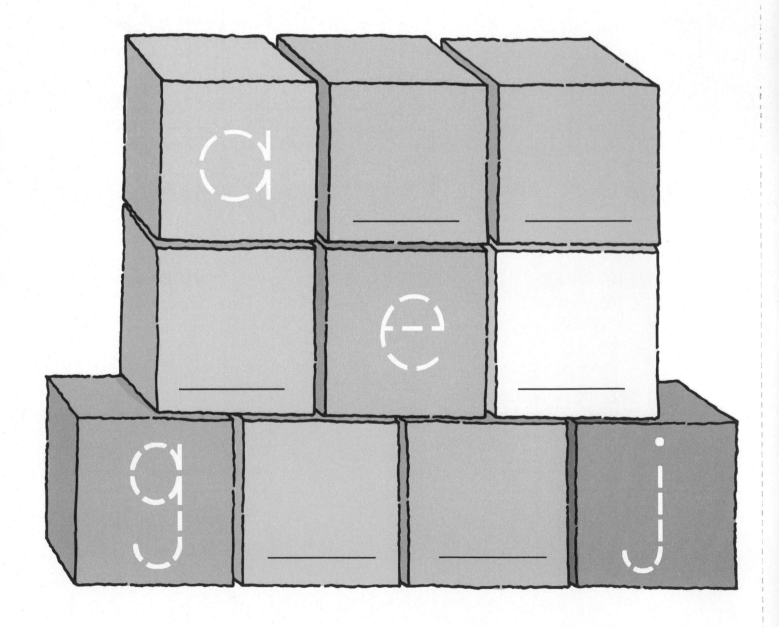

44

LETTER REVIEW

Name_____

Letter U u

Find each hidden **U** and **u**.

Color each **U** purple. **Color** each **u** orange. Then **color** the rest of the picture.

Letter Vv

Name_____

✏️ **Trace** each **V** and **v**.

🖍️ **Color** each heart with **V** or **v** red.

✏️ **Draw** a line from each **V** or **v** to one of the hearts on the left.

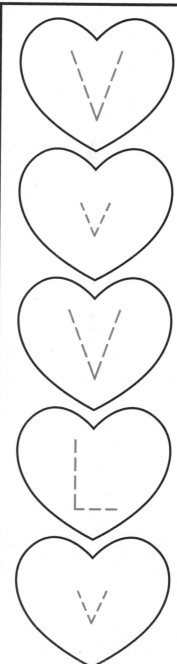

Phonics: Grade Preschool

Letter Ww

Help the spider find its home.

Draw a line to follow each **W** and **w**.
Color the picture.

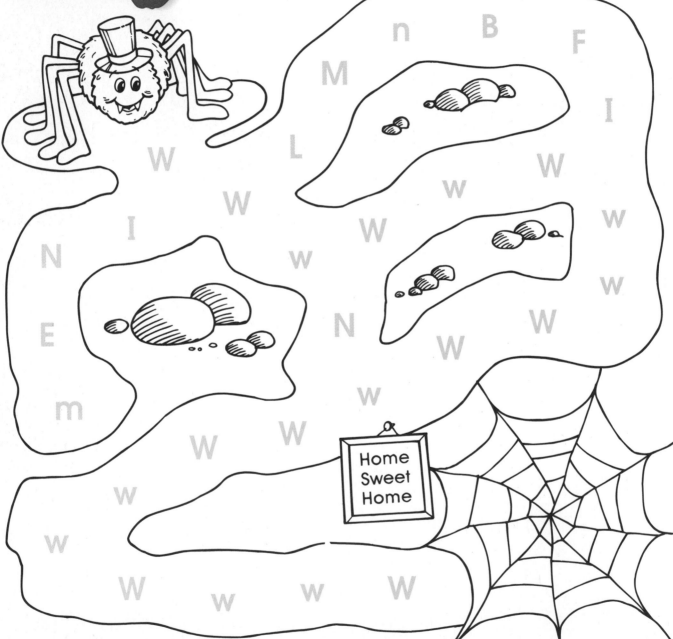

Home Sweet Home

Name_____

Color the **UPPERCASE X**'s **red**. **Color** the lowercase x's **blue**.

For each **UPPERCASE** letter, write its matching **lowercase** letter next to it. For each **lowercase** letter, write its matching **UPPERCASE** letter next to it.

Phonics: Grade Preschool

Name_____

Letter Yy

Find each **Y** and **y** hidden in the yard.

Color each **Y red** and each **y** yellow.
Color the rest of the yard and make it fun!

Name_____

These words start with **Z** or **z**.

✏️ **Write** the **lowercase z** on the line.
Color the pictures. ✏️

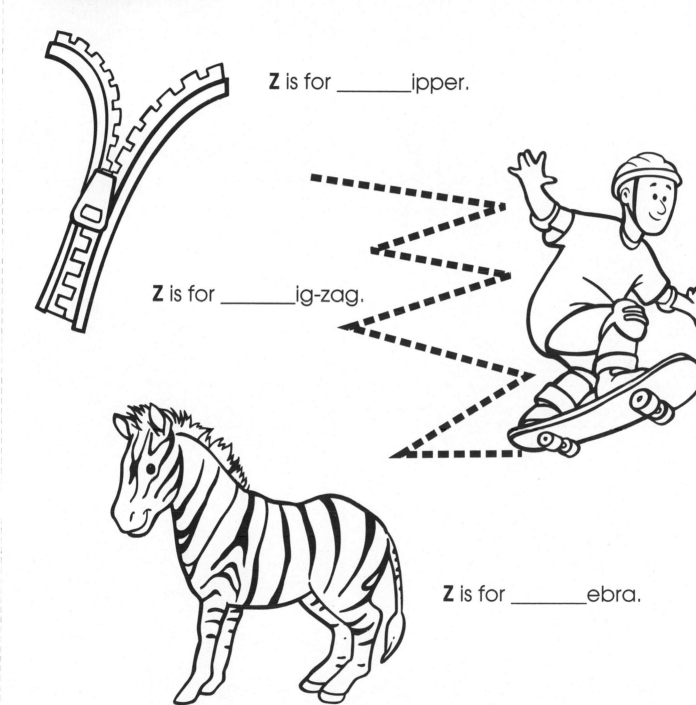

Z is for _____ipper.

Z is for _____ig-zag.

Z is for _____ebra.

Phonics: Grade Preschool

LETTER REVIEW

Name_____

Practice writing the letters **A–Z** below and on pages 53 and 54. Trace the UPPER- and lowercase letters.

Aa Bb

Cc Dd

Ee Ff

Gg Hh

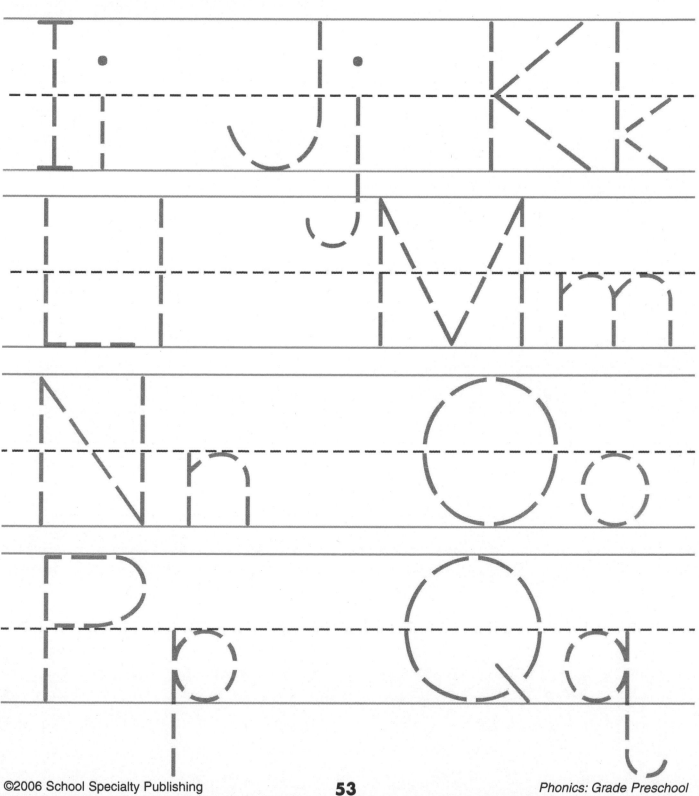

53

LETTER REVIEW

Name_____

BEGINNING SOUNDS

Look at the pictures in each row. Color the picture that has the same beginning sound as the first picture.

BEGINNING SOUNDS

Look at the pictures in each row. Color the picture that has the same beginning sound as the first picture.

Book!

Name_____

Look at the pictures in each row. Color the picture that has the same beginning sound as the first picture.

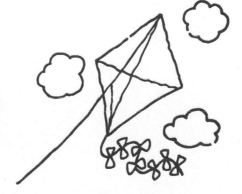

BEGINNING SOUNDS

Name_____

Look at the pictures in each row. Color the picture that has the same beginning sound as the first picture.

 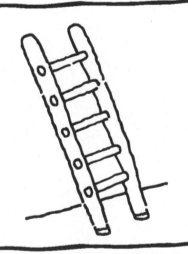 

 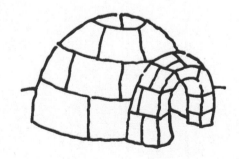 

Name_____

Look at the pictures in each row. Color two pictures in each row that begin with the same sound.

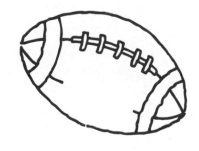  

BEGINNING SOUNDS

Name_____

Look at the pictures in each row. Color two pictures in each row that begin with the same sound.

BEGINNING SOUNDS

Look at the pictures in each row. Color two pictures in each row that begin with the same sound.

Name_____

Look at the pictures in each row. Color two pictures in each row that begin with the same sound.

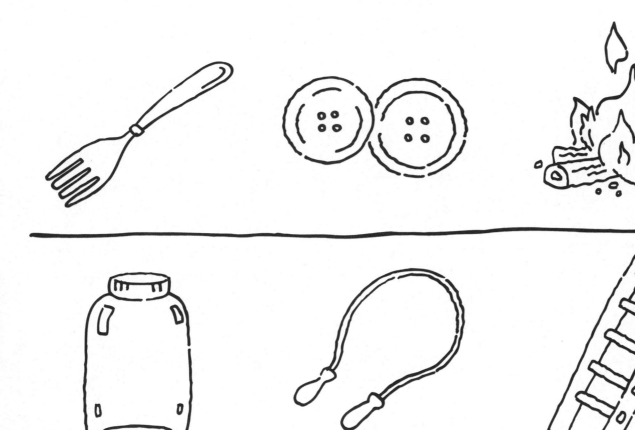

BEGINNING SOUNDS

Name_____

Draw a line from each letter to the picture that begins with that sound.

m

g

o

Phonics: Grade Preschool

BEGINNING SOUNDS

Name_____

Draw a line from each letter to the picture that begins with that sound.

v

z

BEGINNING SOUNDS

Draw a line from each letter to the picture that begins with that sound.

s

y

h

65

Phonics: Grade Preschool

BEGINNING SOUNDS

Draw a line from each letter to the picture that begins with that sound.

a

j

t

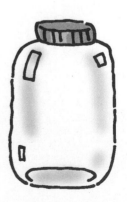

Name_____

Look at the pictures in each row. Color the picture that rhymes with the first picture.

67

RHYMING PICTURES

Name_____

Look at the pictures in each row. Color the picture that rhymes with the first picture.

RHYMING PICTURES

Name_____

Look at the pictures in each row. Color the picture that rhymes with the first picture.

COLORS

Draw a line to match each picture to the crayon with the same color.

3

COLORS

In each row, color two things that are the same color.

4

SAME SIZE

Circle the shape in each row that is the **same size** as the first shape.

9

BIG AND SMALL

Draw a line to match the shapes that are the same. Then color each **big** shape red and each **small** shape green.

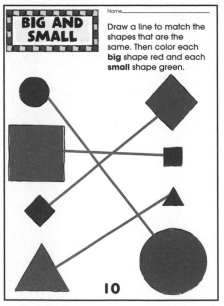

10

OPPOSITES

Look at the pictures in each row. Circle the picture that is the opposite of the first picture in each row.

11

GO-TOGETHERS

Look at the pictures in each row. Circle the picture that goes together with the first picture.

12

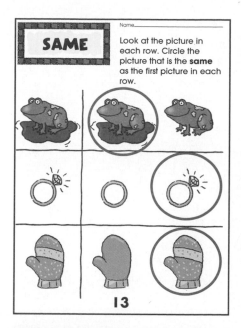

SAME

Name_____

Look at the picture in each row. Circle the picture that is the **same** as the first picture in each row.

13

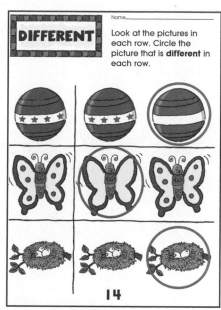

DIFFERENT

Name_____

Look at the pictures in each row. Circle the picture that is **different** in each row.

14

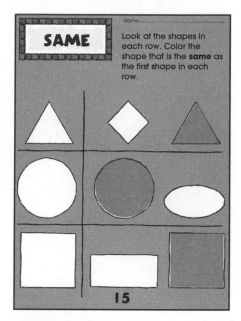

SAME

Name_____

Look at the shapes in each row. Color the shape that is the **same** as the first shape in each row.

15

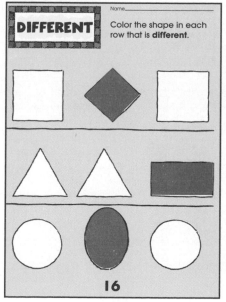

DIFFERENT

Color the shape in each row that is **different**.

16

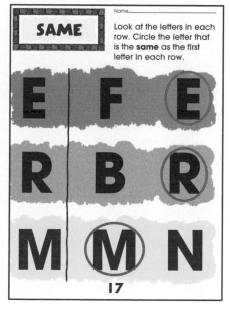

SAME

Name_____

Look at the letters in each row. Circle the letter that is the **same** as the first letter in each row.

17

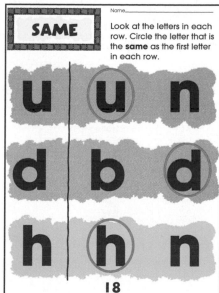

SAME

Name_____

Look at the letters in each row. Circle the letter that is the **same** as the first letter in each row.

18

Phonics: Grade Preschool

Aa

Name_____

Color the **A's red**.
Color the **a's green**.
Color the other letters **yellow**.

19

Bb

Name_____

Color to find the hidden picture.
- Color the spaces with **B blue**.
- Color the spaces with **b yellow**.
- Color the other spaces with a color you like.

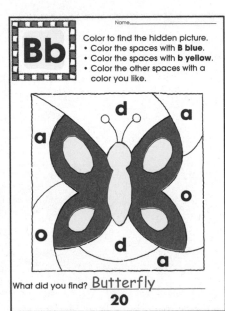

What did you find? __Butterfly__

20

Cc

Name_____

Look at the patterns on the cats' sweaters. Draw a line between the cats with matching **Cc** patterns on their sweaters.

21

LETTER REVIEW

Name_____

Look at the letter each person is holding. Circle the same letter in each box.

22

Dd

Name_____

Help the dolphin jump through the rings. Color the rings that have the letter **D** or **d** in them.

23

Ee

Name_____

Help the baby elephant get to its mother. Color the footprints with **E** or **e** on them.

24

LETTER REVIEW

Name_____

Trace the letters on the caterpillar. Write the missing letters where they belong.

25

Ff

Name_____

Color the fish in the fish bowl.
- Color the **F** fish **orange**.
- Color the **f** fish **green**.
- Color the other fish with a color you like.

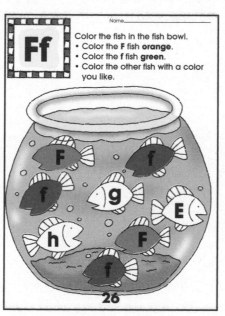

26

Gg

Name_____

Color to find the hidden picture.
- Color the spaces with **G yellow**.
- Color the spaces with **g brown**.

What did you find? Goose

27

Hh

Name_____

Color to find the hidden picture.
- Color the spaces with **H blue**.
- Color the spaces with **h brown**.

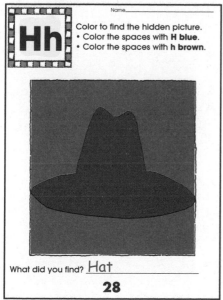

What did you find? Hat

28

Ii

Name_____

Help build the igloo. Trace the letters **I** and **i** below.

29

LETTER REVIEW

Name_____

Trace the letters on the teddy bears. Write the missing letters where they belong.

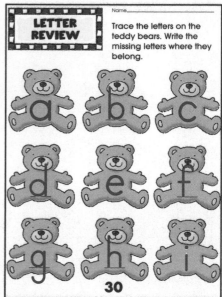

30

Jj

Name_____

Jim has a ticket for a ride. Color to find the hidden picture.
• Color the spaces with **J** or **j** **blue**.
• Color the other spaces **gray**.

What will Jim ride in? _Jet_

31

Kk

Name_____

Look at the letters on each key and lock. Draw a line between the keys and locks with matching letters.

32

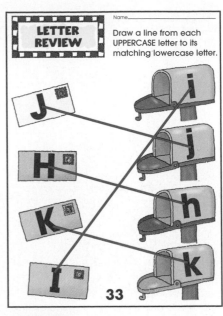

LETTER REVIEW

Name_____

Draw a line from each UPPERCASE letter to its matching lowercase letter.

33

Letter **Ll**

It is fun to rake the fall leaves!
Color the leaves with **L** orange. Color the leaves with **l** red.

34

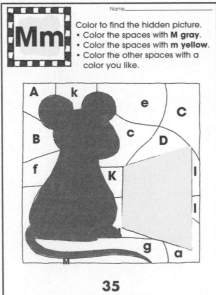

Mm

Name_____

Color to find the hidden picture.
• Color the spaces with **M** gray.
• Color the spaces with **m** yellow.
• Color the other spaces with a color you like.

35

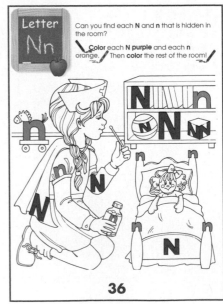

Letter **Nn**

Can you find each **N** and **n** that is hidden in the room?
Color each **N** purple and each **n** orange. Then color the rest of the room!

36

Oo

Name_____

What did the octopus see on the ocean floor?
- Color the spaces with **O** or **o** **blue**.
- Color the other spaces **brown**.

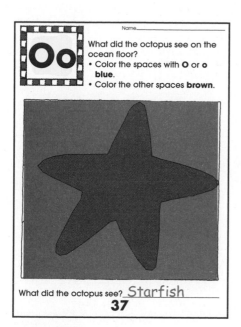

What did the octopus see? _Starfish_

37

Letter Pp

Color each **P** or **p** on the pizza red. Then **color** the rest of the pizza.

38

Name_____

Connect the dots as you say the alphabet from **A** to **P**. Then color the picture.

39

Qq

Name_____

Color the quilt.
- Color the squares with **Q** **green**.
- Color the squares with **q** **pink**.

40

Letter Rr

Trace each **R** and **r**. **Color** each raindrop with **R** green. **Color** each raindrop with **r** blue. Use the same colors for the letters on the umbrella.

41

Ss

Name_____

Look at the letter patterns on the shirts and shorts. Draw a line from each shirt to the pair of shorts with the same letter pattern.

42

Phonics: Grade Preschool

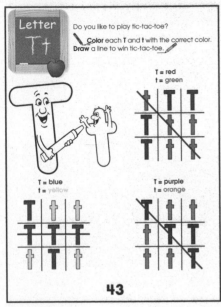

Letter T t

Do you like to play tic-tac-toe?

✏ **Color** each **T** and **t** with the correct color.
Draw a line to win tic-tac-toe. ✏

T = red
t = green

T = blue
t = yellow

T = purple
t = orange

43

LETTER REVIEW

Trace the letters on the blocks. Write the missing letters where they belong below and on page 45.

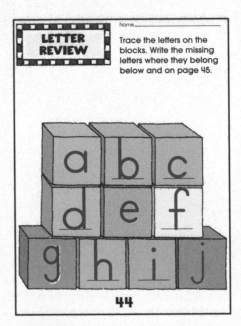

44

LETTER REVIEW

45

Letter U u

Find each hidden **U** and **u**.

✏ **Color** each **U** purple. ✏ **Color** each **u** orange. Then **color** the rest of the picture. ✏

46

Letter V v

✏ **Trace** each **V** and **v**.

✏ **Color** each heart with **V** or **v** red.

✏ **Draw** a line from each **V** or **v** to one of the hearts on the left.

47

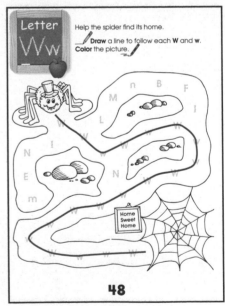

Letter W w

Help the spider find its home.

✏ **Draw** a line to follow each **W** and **w**. **Color** the picture. ✏

Home Sweet Home

48

Letter Xx

Color the UPPERCASE X's red. Color the lowercase x's blue.

For each UPPERCASE letter, write its matching lowercase letter next to it. For each lowercase letter, write its matching UPPERCASE letter next to it.

49

Letter Yy

Find each Y and y hidden in the yard.

Color each Y red and each y yellow. Color the rest of the yard and make it fun!

50

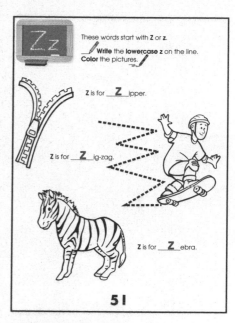

Zz

These words start with Z or z.

Write the lowercase z on the line. Color the pictures.

Z is for __Z__ipper.

Z is for __Z__ig-zag.

Z is for __Z__ebra.

51

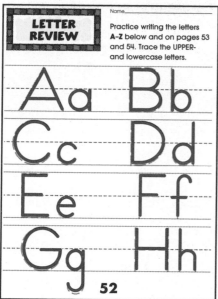

LETTER REVIEW

Name_____

Practice writing the letters A-Z below and on pages 53 and 54. Trace the UPPER- and lowercase letters.

Aa Bb
Cc Dd
Ee Ff
Gg Hh

52

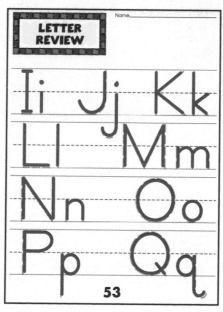

LETTER REVIEW

Name_____

Ii Jj Kk
Ll Mm
Nn Oo
Pp Qq

53

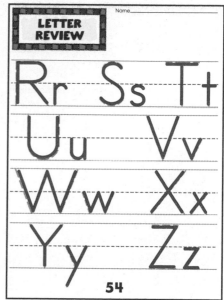

LETTER REVIEW

Name_____

Rr Ss Tt
Uu Vv
Ww Xx
Yy Zz

54

Phonics: Grade Preschool

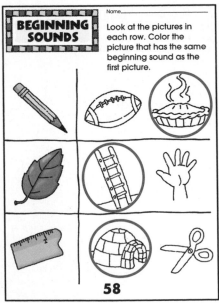

BEGINNING SOUNDS

Name_____

Look at the pictures in each row. Color two pictures in each row that begin with the same sound.

61

BEGINNING SOUNDS

Name_____

Look at the pictures in each row. Color two pictures in each row that begin with the same sound.

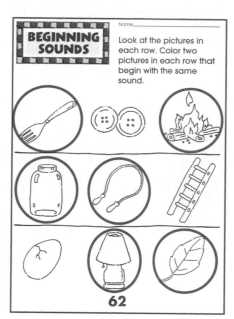

62

BEGINNING SOUNDS

Name_____

Draw a line from each letter to the picture that begins with that sound.

63

BEGINNING SOUNDS

Name_____

Draw a line from each letter to the picture that begins with that sound.

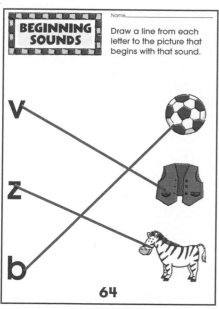

64

BEGINNING SOUNDS

Name_____

Draw a line from each letter to the picture that begins with that sound.

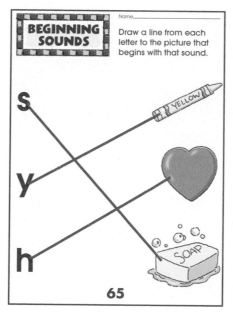

65

BEGINNING SOUNDS

Name_____

Draw a line from each letter to the picture that begins with that sound.

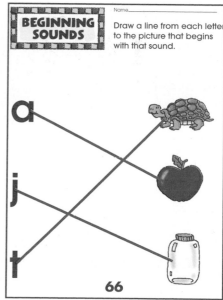

66

Phonics: Grade Preschool